Conscious Collaboration
Mindful Teamwork for Best Results

Table of Contents

1. Introduction 1

2. The Foundation of Conscious Collaboration 2

    2.1. What is Conscious Collaboration? 2

    2.2. Principle of Presence 3

    2.3. Principle of Inclusion 3

    2.4. Principle of Communication 4

    2.5. Principle of Shared Vision 4

    2.6. Tools for Conscious Collaboration 5

    2.7. A Human-Centric Approach 6

3. Awakening Mindfulness in Teamwork 8

    3.1. The Power of Mindfulness 8

    3.2. Laying the Foundations of Mindfulness 9

    3.3. Creating a Culture of Mindful Teamwork 9

    3.4. Overcoming the Challenges to Mindful Teamwork 10

    3.5. Harnessing the Power of Mindful Teamwork 10

4. Building Blocks of Trust and Respect 12

    4.1. Understanding Trust and Respect 12

    4.2. The Importance of Trust and Respect 12

    4.3. Developing Trust 13

    4.4. Cultivating Respect 14

    4.5. Maintaining Trust and Respect 14

5. Active Listening: The Key to Empathetic Teams 16

    5.1. Deep Dive into Active Listening 16

    5.2. Genesis of Empathy through Active Listening 17

    5.3. Techniques for Mastering Active Listening 17

    5.4. Active Listening: Unleashing Team Synergy 18

    5.5. Turning Active Listening into a Habit 18

    5.6. The Resounding Impact of Active Listening 19

6. Emotional Intelligence: The Unsung Hero in Team Dynamics . . . 20

    6.1. The Essence of Emotional Intelligence 20

    6.2. Emotional Intelligence in Team Dynamics 21

    6.3. Enhancing Team Emotional Intelligence 22

7. Improving Communication for Deeper Connections 23

    7.1. The Basics of Communication 23

    7.2. Building Empathy through Active Listening 24

    7.3. Non-Verbal Communication 24

    7.4. The Power of Positive Phrasing 25

    7.5. Conclusion 25

8. The Art of Giving and Receiving Feedback Mindfully 26

    8.1. The Power of Mindful Feedback 26

    8.2. The Act of Giving Feedback Mindfully 26

    8.3. The Grace of Receiving Feedback Mindfully 27

    8.4. Framing Feedback Sessions Mindfully 28

    8.5. Practice Makes Perfect 28

9. Conflict Resolution: A Conscious Way Forward 30

    9.1. Understanding Conflict 30

    9.2. Types of Conflict 30

    9.3. Embracing Conflict as a Constructive Force 31

    9.4. Conflict Resolution: A Conscious Approach 31

    9.5. Active Listening 31

    9.6. Empathetic Communication 32

    9.7. Problem-Solving Together 32

    9.8. Building a Conflict Resolution Framework 32

    9.9. Integrating Conscious Collaboration in Conflict Resolution . . 32

10. The Science Behind Peak Performance 34

    10.1. The Mind-Body Connection 34

    10.2. Biochemical Players 35

    10.3. The Role of Psychological Factors and Positive

Affirmations 35

10.4. Conscious Collaboration: The Crucial Link 36

10.5. A Culture of Learning for Performance 37

11. Sustaining Conscious Collaboration for Long Haul Success 38

11.1. The Importance of Nurturing Conscious Collaboration 38

11.2. Continual Reinforcement of Collaborative Principles 38

11.3. Building Empathy within the Team 39

11.4. Encouraging Active Listening 39

11.5. Promoting Respect and Shared Ambition 40

11.6. Review and Adaptation of Conscious Collaboration
Practices 40

11.7. Measuring Success and Addressing Failures 40

11.8. Conclusion: Sustaining Conscious Collaboration — A
Continuous Endeavor 41

Chapter 1. Introduction

Get ready to dive into the captivating world of Conscious Collaboration! This Special Report delves into the art of mindful teamwork and how it can supercharge your team performance, unleash creativity, and elevate business results. Imagine transforming your work environment into a symphony of synergies where every participant is not just mechanically 'doing their part', but truly engaged, aware, and contributing to a harmonious collective. Do you aspire to a work culture filled with enhanced empathy, active listening, profound respect, and shared ambitions? If so, this Special Report is your golden ticket. Pleasant and cheerful in its approach, yet backed by rigorous research, it's not just an enlightening read, but a handbook for success. Take a step towards extraordinary team dynamism today and illuminate your path to commendable achievements!

Chapter 2. The Foundation of Conscious Collaboration

Establishing the underpinnings of conscious collaboration requires a thorough understanding of the key concepts, principles, and tools that comprise its foundation. Embracing a more mindful form of teamwork, as professed by conscious collaboration, can fuel creativity within a team, heighten productivity, and yield impressive results.

2.1. What is Conscious Collaboration?

Conscious collaboration is an approach that combines individual mindful awareness with collective action and cohesion. Despite their differences, members of a consciously collaborating team skillfully coordinate their actions to serve the common objective, underpinned by a robust web of awareness and understanding of individual roles and responsibilities.

This collaborative model's uniqueness lies in its emphasis on mindfulness: the sentient, active presence in the moment, enabling individuals to engage fully with their tasks and team dynamics. The conscious collaborator is both an observer and participant, bringing a different level of attention and intention to their role, enhancing their contribution to collective efforts.

Several principles come together to define this form of collaboration, providing a fundamental guide for the application of conscious collaboration in everyday teamwork.

2.2. Principle of Presence

'Presence' forms the bedrock of conscious collaboration. It represents the ability to be fully aware and engaged in the present moment, free from distractions or preoccupations hovering in your mind. It's this total immersion that allows a collaborator to contribute optimally to the collective.

Presence enhances the ability to perceive the nuances of team dynamics. With full awareness of a situation, an individual can contribute more effectively, respond intelligently to shifts in trends or occurrences, and thus make a significant difference.

This principle encourages individuals to put aside their personal preoccupations, thereby enabling them to tune in to the requirements of the task at hand and the overall goal of the collaborative effort, promoting alignment with the collaborative intent.

2.3. Principle of Inclusion

The principle of inclusion underpins the belief that every member of a team brings valuable capabilities, perspectives, and ideas to the collective. Conscious collaboration encourages diversity, recognizing that it's this amalgam of skills and insights that leads to fertile, creative problem-solving and innovation.

Inclusion fosters a sense of belonging, instilling the belief in each member that they matter to the team and that their contribution has an impact. When members feel inclusive, they are more likely to contribute their authentic thoughts and ideas, pushing the team's creative boundaries and boosting efforts towards achieving shared goals.

2.4. Principle of Communication

Central to conscious collaboration is the principle of communication. Authentic, honest, transparent communication fortifies trust within the team, making collaboration more seamless and effective. Good communication breaks down barriers, builds understanding, and promotes the sharing of ideas.

This principle encourages open dialogue, active listening, and expressing thoughts with honesty and respect. A consciously collaborating team uses communication to cultivate a safe environment where ideas and difference of opinion can be expressed fearlessly but respectfully, leading to the emergence of innovation and shared understanding.

2.5. Principle of Shared Vision

In conscious collaboration, a shared vision binds the team together. Connected by common goals and aspirations, team members work towards fulfilling their shared objectives. A shared vision promotes commitment, driving the team towards achieving collective successes, while acknowledging and respecting individual contributions.

Using these principles as stepping stones, teams can lay the groundwork for robust, mindful, and conscious collaboration that leads to elevated performance, creativity, and outstanding results. But understanding these principles is just part of the equation - it's the application of these principles that lays the foundation for conscious collaboration.

2.6. Tools for Conscious Collaboration

To assist in the practical application of conscious collaboration, several tools can help imbibe these principles into everyday teamwork.

- Mindfulness meditation: This practice cultivates an individual's ability to remain present, intentional, and non-judgmental. Regular practice helps to enhance listening skills, empathy, and patience, thereby benefitting the teamwork experience.

- Open dialogue: Engaging in open conversations promotes transparency and trust among team members. When everyone feels heard and respected, collaboration becomes significantly more effective.

- Appreciative Inquiry: This tool promotes a focus on strengths and opportunities rather than problems. Used in team scenarios, it enables a collective orientation towards success, fostering positivity, engagement, and successful outcomes.

- Empathy mapping: By visualizing what team members might be thinking, feeling, and experiencing, this tool enhances understanding and fosters a more empathetic team environment.

Imbibing and infusing the principles of conscious collaboration into everyday operations won't happen overnight. It is a journey that requires consistent effort, encouragement, training, and commitment. But once these foundational stones are laid, the path to a highly collaborative, harmonious, and productive work culture becomes accessible.

However, it's important to remember the human element in conscious collaboration. Behind every participant's role, there's an individual who brings their unique blend of experiences, beliefs, ideas, and emotions. Recognizing and addressing this individuality is a vital aspect of fostering conscious collaboration.

2.7. A Human-Centric Approach

Conscious collaboration embraces a human-centric ethos. It appreciates that it's the individuals who make the team, and therefore, identifies and acknowledges their individual strengths, weaknesses, skills, and competencies.

A human-centric approach nurtures an environment where the team members feel valued, heard, and at ease to share their ideas without fear of criticism or judgment. Such an atmosphere fosters creativity, innovation, and mutual support, which are the cornerstones of a robust collaborative organization.

Achieving conscious collaboration involves purposeful effort towards creating a trusting and inclusive environment where conscious communication, shared vision, and mindful action are fostered. Laying this foundation will set the stage for a collaborative work culture that drives individual satisfaction and superior team performance.

Despite these comprehensive guidelines, practical difficulties and challenges are inevitable. Cognitive biases, communication breakdowns, or conflict can mar the collaborative process. But as we know, challenges are also opportunities for learning, strengthening, and refining. Stay mindful, stay committed, and remember that each setback is just another stepping stone on the path to conscious collaboration.

Understanding these foundational elements is a step towards transforming your team into a high-functioning, harmonious entity, better equipped to handle the complexities of modern work. The journey is not a sprint but a marathon. But every step taken in the right direction is a step closer to achieving the extraordinariness of a consciously collaborating team. Embrace the potential that lies in conscious collaboration and steer your team towards a future of shared success.

Chapter 3. Awakening Mindfulness in Teamwork

The realm of teamwork has constantly evolved through centuries; from being a necessity for survival during prehistoric eras to being a crucial asset in driving business success in the modern corporate world. In today's interconnected and rapidly changing work environment, a team's ability to operate efficiently, creatively, and empathetically can set the stage for its ultimate success or failure. While having members with requisite skills is integral, inducing a consciously collaborative state - a state of mindful teamwork - is the secret to extraordinary team accomplishment. Let's embark on the journey of awakening mindfulness in teamwork.

3.1. The Power of Mindfulness

Mindfulness: an ancient art cultivated thousands of years ago, is gaining new traction in the modern corporate world. It is the practice of deliberately paying attention, non-judgmentally, to the experience arising in the present moment. A state of active, open, intentional attention to the present, when applied to the team working environment, can lead to remarkable outcomes.

When individuals deploy mindfulness, the effects are potent - improved focus, stress reduction, increase in emotional intelligence, enhanced cognitive flexibility, and improved relationship satisfaction. Therefore, it's not surprising that amplifying this effect across a team by nurturing mindfulness at a collective level could radically enhance work dynamics.

3.2. Laying the Foundations of Mindfulness

So how does one instill this sense of purposeful awareness in a team?

Understanding the importance of mindfulness: The practice begins with understanding its implications for not just individuals but also the team as a whole. Teams need to comprehend how conscious collaboration enhances empathy, active listening, mutual respect, and shared ambitions – essentially the raw materials for building a successful team.

Encouraging mindful communication: This involves the members expressing their thoughts, feelings, and expectations clearly and listening actively. It encourages open dialogue and discourages assumptions.

Setting a shared vision and goals: All members should unite behind a shared team vision and work towards its realization. It's not only about understanding individual tasks but also seeing how each contributes to the grand scheme.

3.3. Creating a Culture of Mindful Teamwork

Building a culture of mindfulness does not happen overnight. It is a process that unfolds gradually, requiring constant reinforcement.

Modeling Mindful Behaviour: Leadership plays a crucial role here. When leaders model mindful behaviour - when they listen carefully, show openness to others' ideas, and demonstrate empathy - their actions get mirrored in the team behavior.

Training and Practice: Regular mindfulness exercises such as meditation, mindful listening, or mindful walkthroughs of tasks can be incorporated into the team's routine.

Feedback & Reflection: Regular feedback and a culture of continuous improvement can highlight areas of improvement or success, fostering a conscious, reflective team approach.

3.4. Overcoming the Challenges to Mindful Teamwork

Just like any significant shift in work culture, promoting mindfulness among teams is riddled with challenges - resistance to change, lack of immediate tangible results, or challenges in maintaining consistency.

Addressing Resistance: To overcome resistance, it is important to communicate the intent behind the change and the expected benefits. Transparently discussing potential challenges and solutions can also promote buy-in.

Patience and Persistence: Immediate results are uncommon. A culture of mindfulness takes time to flourish; the key is to persist in training and encouragement.

3.5. Harnessing the Power of Mindful Teamwork

As the team evolves to foster mindful teamwork, countless rewards unveil themselves. The direct correlation between mindfulness and enhanced empathy, eco-centric thinking, active listening, profound respect, and shared ambitions manifests. Teams become more agile to changes and overcome challenges with greater creativity. Conflict and misunderstandings are reduced, while levels of trust and reciprocity mount.

Mindfulness in teamwork truly stands as the game-changer in paving the path to commendable achievements. So, awaken this power within your team and create a harmonious environment for shared success. The tremendous potential of conscious collaboration, once unlocked, can take teams to terrains uncharted and heights unimagined. Congratulations, as you embark on this transformational journey to elevate teamwork, facilitate growth and innovation, and ultimately, change the game of team collaboration forever.

Chapter 4. Building Blocks of Trust and Respect

Trust and respect, the foundational principles of any successful team, act as the nuts and bolts that hold the structure of collaboration together. When team members trust one another, they are fostering a psychologically safe environment where all feel valued, accepted, and free to contribute their ideas without fear of judgment or rejection.

4.1. Understanding Trust and Respect

Before exploring how to build trust and respect in a team setting, it's essential to understand their definitions. Trust is the belief that one can rely upon others, coupled with the expectation that they will act in a consistent, dependable, and supportive manner. Respect is acknowledging the value and worth of others, celebrating their individuality, and treating them with kindness, dignity, and understanding.

Trust and respect are tightly intertwined, and one rarely comes without the other. Respect breeds trust – an individual who displays a respectful, dignified, and considerate attitude towards others is more likely to gain their trust.

4.2. The Importance of Trust and Respect

Trust and respect are the glue that binds a team together. High levels of trust and respect among team members create an open environment where individuals feel comfortable sharing their ideas, communicating honestly, and taking risks. Such environment cultivates innovation and creativity. Moreover, when team members trust and respect each other, they are more likely to be committed to team objectives and work collaboratively towards a shared goal.

Trust and respect provide significant employee benefits, too. It helps to decrease stress, foster satisfaction, and enhance work performance. When employees feel trusted and respected, they are likely to have a positive perception of the work environment, which leads to increased productivity and commitment to the organization.

4.3. Developing Trust

Developing trust within a team involves building relationships, demonstrating consistency, and cultivating an atmosphere of transparency and honesty.

Consistency is the key to helping others feel comfortable and trust in your actions. Team members must feel safe that their peers will react in an expected and predictable manner towards their ideas and contributions. This also applies to team leaders; consistent leadership fosters an environment of stability and relies on learning how to provide constructive feedback, being patient, and showing empathy consistently.

Transparency and honesty are also essential for building trust. Managers must be honest with their team, whether sharing good news or bad. Honesty helps create a transparent environment where team members feel informed and valued, leading to increased trust levels.

Developing relationships play a crucial role as well. Teams build trust by creating connections and getting to know one another better. Techniques such as team-building exercises, open communication and regular check-ins can be beneficial in nurturing these relationships.

4.4. Cultivating Respect

Cultivating respect in a team environment often begins with establishing a culture of empathy and understanding. Encourage team members to understand one another's perspectives and show gratitude towards each other's contributions, promoting an inclusive and diverse atmosphere.

Active listening, practiced by all team members, can help enhance respect within a team. When team members know that their ideas are genuinely heard and valued, it shows respect for them and their inputs.

Modeling respectful behavior is as important. Team leaders must exemplify respectful behavior in their interactions with others, thereby setting the standard for all team members.

Promoting mutual respect can also involve establishing clear guidelines on acceptable behavior within the team, addressing issues openly and constructively when they surface, maintaining a positive and supportive environment and establishing a culture of continual learning and growth.

4.5. Maintaining Trust and Respect

Establishing trust and respect within a team is the beginning. The real challenge lies in maintaining these qualities over time. Open and effective communication, continued displays of trustworthy behavior, and mutual respect should form the core of ongoing team interactions.

Feedback cultures can also support the continued maintenance of trust and respect. Constructive feedback shows that those involved are interested in one another's development and success, reinforcing mutual respect.

Regular check-ins are beneficial too. Assign a designated time for team members to share their thoughts, concerns, or ideas. This allows everyone to feel heard and validated, further bolstering respect and trust.

In summary, trust and respect are not just inherent qualities but can—and should—be actively fostered within a team. They have a profound impact on team dynamics, employee satisfaction, and ultimately, organizational success. Therefore, it's important for organizations to consciously and continuously work upon building and maintaining these crucial building blocks of successful collaborative environments.

Chapter 5. Active Listening: The Key to Empathetic Teams

Understanding the essence of active listening is vital for fostering optimal team dynamics. It not only promotes better understanding among team members but also empowers them to communicate effectively and sympathetically. This chapter focuses on outlining the concept of active listening and examines its critical role in nurturing empathetic teams.

5.1. Deep Dive into Active Listening

The backbone of any fruitful interaction or conversation is effective listening. Active listening, more specifically, is a heightened form of listening that involves consciousness, attentiveness, and complete focus on the speaker, their message, and their opinion. It goes beyond just hearing words; it is about the effort to understand, interpret, and respond constructively.

Active listening is actively absorbing the information given to you by the speaker, showing that you are listening and interested, providing feedback to the speaker to ensure that you are correctly grasifying the information given, and prompting the speaker to continue with small verbal comments and nonverbal cues.

This form of listening is proactive and requires a certain sense of mindfulness in order to be truly effective. It delves deeper than the surface of routine and mechanical listening, plunging into the realms of empathy and connection.

5.2. Genesis of Empathy through Active Listening

Active listening drives empathy in teams by fostering a deeper understanding of individual perspectives. By harnessing this potent tool, you can elevate your personal and professional relationships.

Empathy is the ability to understand and share the feelings of another. It is to step into someone's shoes and see the world from their viewpoint. This emotional intelligence skill, when twinned with active listening, fuels harmonious and impactful team dynamics.

When active listening is applied, the listener seeks to see the world through the speaker's lens. This involves acknowledging emotions, understanding viewpoints, and showcasing genuine interest in their perspective.

5.3. Techniques for Mastering Active Listening

Mastering active listening requires conscious effort. Here are some methods that can help provoke a culture of active listening, nurturing empathetic and efficient teams:

1. Restating: Paraphrase what the speaker has said to ensure understanding.

2. Reflecting: Reflect the speaker's emotions and implications of their message.

3. Questioning: Use open-ended questions to encourage more detailed responses.

4. Clarifying: Ask about specific points to ensure understanding and avoid ambiguity.

5. Summarizing: Recap the key points to confirm the right comprehension of the information.

Through these techniques, not only can we encourage deeper dialogues, but we also actively participate in conversations, keeping them alive and significant.

5.4. Active Listening: Unleashing Team Synergy

When active listening is deeply entrenched in a team's culture, a symphony of synergies gets unveiled. With the automatic undercurrent of understanding and respect, every team member will feel valued and heard.

When the team members actively listen, they foster acknowledgment, encourage patience, boost morale, and significantly decrease any misunderstanding. This phenomenon paves the way for empathetic teams that are bound together by a comprehensive fabric of mutual understanding, respect, and shared ambitions.

5.5. Turning Active Listening into a Habit

To truly harness the power of active listening, it must be transformed into a habit – a part of the team's cultural DNA. It is not a one-time effort but an ongoing process that requires commitment.

From daily standups to monthly company-wide meetings, integrate active listening into every possible facet of team interaction. Training sessions, workshops, and roleplays can inculcate the essence of active listening among the team.

As active listening becomes an unconscious habit within the team, it starts reflecting in the collective results. This journey from conscious effort to unconscious habit is the golden path to forming empathetic teams.

5.6. The Resounding Impact of Active Listening

With active listening as the anchor, the landscape of teamwork evolves. Teams become more collaborative, empathetic, and effective - a transformation laying the groundwork for supercharged performance and elevated business results.

Active listening fosters an atmosphere of trust and personal connection within the team. This work environment, characterized by enhanced empathy, active listening, profound respect, and shared ambitions, is ultimately the fertile soil where success grows.

In conclusion, active listening is much more than a communication tool. It is the key to unlocking empathetic teams, building stronger and more meaningful relationships, and driving success. Cultivating this craft can indeed lead to an exceptionally harmonious and effective working environment. So, let us invest time and effort in honing this essential skill and witness the radical transformation in our teams.

Chapter 6. Emotional Intelligence: The Unsung Hero in Team Dynamics

Every well-accomplished team maintains a secret valve that lets them harmonize their roles, empathize with others, and navigate through conflicts with less friction. That 'secret' is none other than Emotional Intelligence (EI), and it serves as an unsung hero in the dynamics of any team's overall performance.

EI is the ability to understand, use, and manage one's own emotions in positive ways, which involves demonstrating empathy for others, overcoming challenges, and defusing conflict. Emotional Intelligence can influence our productivity, attitude, and how we socialize within and beyond our work environment. It allows us to lead and inspire, collaborate efficiently, and cultivate meaningful relationships.

6.1. The Essence of Emotional Intelligence

Emotional Intelligence is divided into five main components, as outlined by psychologist and author Daniel Goleman: self-awareness, self-regulation, motivation, empathy, and social skills. Each is integral in enhancing our ability to work effectively within a team.

Self-awareness is the recognition of our own emotions and their impact on our actions and decisions. It's about understanding our strengths and weaknesses, and having self-confidence.

Self-regulation involves managing our emotions, being adaptable, following through on commitments, and resisting inappropriate or impulsive behaviors.

Motivation is the drive to achieve beyond expectations, both ours and others'. It's about being passionate about our work, and it's unaffected by financial gains.

Empathy is being aware of, understanding and appreciating the feelings of others. It's about taking an active interest in their concerns, understanding and learning from their perspective.

Finally, social skills consist of managing relationships to move people into the desired direction, being an effective communicator, and being good at managing change, conflict, and building bonds.

6.2. Emotional Intelligence in Team Dynamics

Emotionally intelligent teams are able to manage and harness emotions for the collective success of the group. Here are three ways how Emotional Intelligence infuses itself into team dynamics:

1. Conflict Resolution: Conflicts are natural when individuals with different perspectives and approaches come together. EI empowers teams to navigate conflicts smoothly and come to mutual resolutions. Rather than letting heated emotions cloud judgment, team members use understanding, empathy, and open-mindedness to solve conflicts, creating a more harmonious work environment.

2. Team Cooperation: Emotionally intelligent team members encourage a culture of respect, understanding, and equality. They are attuned to the emotions of others and respond with empathy and consideration. This fosters a sense of trust and togetherness in the team relationship, and promotes cooperation and collaboration.

3. Increase in Performance: When team members are emotionally intelligent, they are better equipped to manage their own

emotions and reactions. They understand the motivations and actions of their peers better, which promotes an environment that is stress-free and pleasant - a perfect recipe for improved productivity and performance.

6.3. Enhancing Team Emotional Intelligence

Improving the team's emotional intelligence can lead to improved relationships, increase collaboration, and ultimately drive a high-performance culture. Here are some practical ways to enhance the team's emotional intelligence:

Training and development: This is a great way of enhancing emotional intelligence within the team. Regular EI trainings and workshops can be beneficial as they provide the necessary tools and resources for team members to learn and grow.

Regular feedbacks: Provide consistent and constructive feedback. This helps team members to recognize their strengths and areas of improvement. Moreover, it allows a space for team members to express and understand their emotions, which promotes self-awareness and empathy within the team.

Creating a culture of trust: For emotional intelligence to thrive, it's imperative to build a foundation of trust in the team. Honest conversations, open communication, and mutual respect are ways to establish and maintain such culture.

Emotional Intelligence is not a soft skill, but a key leadership competency that affects the bottom line. It might feel uncomfortable and challenging to incorporate emotional intelligence into daily work life initially. However, consistent effort, an open mind, and patience can bring about significant shifts in the team dynamics.

Chapter 7. Improving Communication for Deeper Connections

Good communication lies at the heart of building strong, significant, and lasting relationships. It's the conduit that facilitates understanding, trust, empathy, and, ultimately, efficiency in a team.

To improve our intra-team communication for deeper connections, this writing will break down into multiple sub-parts: The Basics of Communication, Building Empathy through Active Listening, Non-Verbal Communication, and The Power of Positive Phrasing.

7.1. The Basics of Communication

Communication starts with the understanding that it's a two-way street. It implies that we express our ideas, feelings, and thoughts, and simultaneously listen and comprehend other's perspectives and emotions. It is not a monologue but rather an engaging dialogue, an exchange of energies and understandings. Remember that everyone communicates differently; being mindful of these differences can enhance the ability of your team to collaborate.

A key part of effective communication is clarity. Ambiguity can result in misunderstanding and potentially harmful errors. Always ensure that your message is fully understood, simpler language can often be more effective to ensure everyone is on the same page. Framing your thought in an unambiguous, straightforward manner helps evade possible areas of confusion and create a smoother communication flow.

7.2. Building Empathy through Active Listening

Empathy isn't just about understanding another's feelings; it's about communicating and acknowledging that understanding. This makes active listening an instrumental part of empathetic communication. While the speaker is communicating their thoughts, as a listener, you have the responsibility to sincerely make an effort to understand the emotions involved, rather than just passively hearing.

Active listening requires you to refrain from merely formulating your response while the other person is speaking. Instead, fully concentrate on the speaker, showing your interest through various cues like nodding, affirmative sounds, and paraphrasing their statements for better understanding and reflection. This not only increases the trust and respect between the parties, but it can also lead to deeper connections.

7.3. Non-Verbal Communication

Non-verbal cues often carry weight that exceeds the spoken words. Facial expressions, eye contact, body movement, and gestures tacitly convey emotions and attitudes, making interpretation a crucial part of comprising effective communication skills.

In a team environment, always maintain positive and open body language. It can signify your openness to others' ideas and foster an atmosphere conducive to open discourse. Understanding and appropriately responding to non-verbal signals can bridge gaps that may form due to miscommunication, creating a more effective and harmonious team environment.

7.4. The Power of Positive Phrasing

How we phrase our words matters significantly, particularly when dealing with complex situations or sensitive matters. A crucial tool in the communication toolbox, positive phrasing transforms potential confrontations into constructive dialogues.

When giving feedback, try to use phrases like 'I noticed' or 'Could we try' instead of direct negative comments. This approach leads to problem-solving discussions rather than confrontational arguments, thus maintaining a mutually respectful environment.

7.5. Conclusion

Commendable communication is a combination of understanding the basics, empathetic listening, reading and projecting appropriate non-verbal cues, and using positive phrasing. Respecting and understanding these facets will guide your team to heightened collaboration, greater trust, and deeper connections. This cultural shift won't happen overnight, but rest assured, incremental changes will lead to a transformative and synergistically efficient team dynamic. Commit yourselves to this approach to communication, and not only will your team benefit but your collective work will be significantly enhanced.

Remember, communication is the essential lifeblood of any functioning team. Treat it with the seriousness and respect it deserves, and your team will surely unlock new peaks of efficiency, productivity, and satisfaction. Only then can you say, in all honesty, that you have truly mastered the art of Conscious Collaboration.

Chapter 8. The Art of Giving and Receiving Feedback Mindfully

Feedback is a crucial aspect of any work environment. It drives improvement, fosters communication, and inspires growth. However, the art of giving and receiving feedback mindfully goes beyond these basic functions. It transforms feedback from a mere process to an enlightening experience that not just points out the flaws but also celebrates the strengths and encourages development.

8.1. The Power of Mindful Feedback

The power of mindful feedback lies in its ability to shift the focus from 'what is wrong' to 'how can we make this even better'. It doesn't seek to criticize, but to understand and nurture. Instead of generating defensiveness or discouragement, it fuels positive change and growth, making it one of the most effective tools for overall team performance enhancement.

Encouraging a mindful feedback culture takes conscious effort. Openheartedness, patience, understanding, and respect form its pillars. This practice is not about blanket appreciated or mindless condemnation; it's about genuine recognition of one's efforts and constructive input to help them soar higher.

8.2. The Act of Giving Feedback Mindfully

Giving feedback can be daunting, but doing it mindfully can turn the tables. To communicate effectively and foster understanding, it's important to refrain from letting emotions run the show. Breathing exercises or brief moments of silence before delivering feedback can help cool down heated emotions, thus enabling a clear and considerate approach.

- Constructive, Not Critical: Begin stating the positives alongside the areas that need improvement. Instead of pointing fingers, use constructive language and examples to illustrate your points. This encourages dialogue rather than argument.

- Specificity and Clarity: Be clear and concise about the feedback. Instead of vague complaints, present constructive suggestions.

- Feedback is a Dialogue: Encourage open communication. Request for their view on the matter, creating an environment of mutual respect and understanding.

8.3. The Grace of Receiving Feedback Mindfully

Receiving feedback is a vulnerable moment that can foster growth if approached with an open mind. Here are a few pointers to receive feedback mindfully.

- Active Listening: Maintaining eye contact, nodding, and acknowledging the speaker's points respects their effort at offering feedback and demonstrates your willingness to learn and grow.

- Embrace Negativity With Positivity: Instead of resisting negative feedback, acknowledge it with grace. See it as an opportunity to learn and improve.

- Ask Questions, Seek Clarity: If you're unsure about anything, ask for clarification. It shows that you are genuinely interested in bettering yourself and not just superficially accepting the feedback.

8.4. Framing Feedback Sessions Mindfully

Designing mindful feedback sessions can help in regulating the process and manage emotional triggers during these sessions. The setting matters a lot; it should be calm, neutral, and devoid of distractions.

Set a specific time for feedback. Make it clear that it is a dialogue and not an attack or a lecture. To reduce defensiveness, you can start with a positive statement about the individual's contribution and then move onto areas of improvement.

===The Impact of Mindful Feedback on Team Relationships

Mindful feedback cultivates a culture of respect, understanding, and mutual growth. A team with a mindful feedback culture enjoys stronger bonds, improved communication, and increased productivity. Plus, it transforms the workplace into a space for collective and individual learning, where mistakes are seen as opportunities, not failures.

8.5. Practice Makes Perfect

Like every skill, mastering the art of mindful feedback takes practice. Begin by practicing mindfulness in everyday life, like being fully present during conversations, acknowledging your own emotions, and being receptive to diverse perspectives. Apply these mindfulness practices during feedback sessions to gradually build and nurture a culture of mindful feedback at your workplace.

Overall, the art of giving and receiving feedback mindfully is all about fostering understanding, respect, and growth. It's a transformational process that enriches team culture, work relationships, and individual skills, paving the path for extraordinary achievements.

Implement these strategies and observe your team dynamics change for the better. Embrace mindfulness in feedback sessions to transform your workplace environment into a haven of understanding, collaboration, and growth. After all, the strength of the team lies in each individual, and the strength of each individual lies in the team.

Chapter 9. Conflict Resolution: A Conscious Way Forward

Modern business workplaces are microcosms of society, brimming with diverse individuals pooling their talents towards common goals. However, with diversity comes inevitable conflict. In such instances, transforming conflicts into opportunities for growth becomes pivotal. This transformation can be achieved through conscious collaboration, which guides us towards mindfulness and empathy, and ultimately, effective conflict resolution.

9.1. Understanding Conflict

Before diving into resolution strategies, it's crucial to understand what conflict really is. Conflict is a situation where two or more individuals perceive their ideas, thoughts, or needs as incompatible. This perceived incompatibility might stem from differences in values, goals, or the methods of achieving those goals. Recognizing conflict is the first conscious step towards resolution.

9.2. Types of Conflict

Generally, conflicts can be classified into the following categories:

1. Task conflict - related to the goals of the work or different viewpoints on how to achieve those goals.

2. Relationship conflict - rooted in personal differences, such as values, personality traits, or lifestyle preferences.

3. Process conflict - concerns about the policies, practices, or norms that govern how team members work together.

While task and process conflicts, if managed correctly, can boost creativity and strengthen team cohesion, relationship conflicts are typically detrimental. Consciously distinguishing between these types is a crucial step towards effective conflict resolution.

9.3. Embracing Conflict as a Constructive Force

Many see conflict as a destructive force. However, when handled consciously and collaboratively, it can become a catalyst for team growth. Conflict brings up diverse perspectives, stimulates creativity, enhances decision-making, and ultimately leads to more satisfying solutions. Being open to conflict can transform a potential problem into a valuable learning opportunity.

9.4. Conflict Resolution: A Conscious Approach

Now that we understand conflict better, let's move onto adopting a conscious approach towards resolving it. A conscious approach is built on mindfulness, empathy, respect, and shared ambitions. It focuses on the 'why' behind the conflict and works actively to mend differences rather than just pacifying the situation superficially.

9.5. Active Listening

Active listening is a cornerstone of the conscious approach to conflict resolution. It requires team members to listen carefully, empathize, and understand fully before responding. This prevents the escalation of disagreements and helps avoid misunderstandings that can intensify the conflict. Encouraging active listening nurtures a supportive environment conducive to harmony and collaboration.

9.6. Empathetic Communication

Empathy allows individuals to see the conflict from the other's perspective, leading to more balanced and fair resolutions. Empathetic communication requires intentionality. It actively seeks to understand, validate, and respect the feelings of others, thereby diffusing tension and fostering deeper connections.

9.7. Problem-Solving Together

Effective conflict resolution is not about winning or losing; it's about collaboratively finding a solution that satisfies everyone. This requires setting aside personal biases, actively engaging in dialogue and negotiation, focusing on shared objectives, and working together to create win-win solutions.

9.8. Building a Conflict Resolution Framework

A well-defined conflict resolution framework guides teams in managing and transforming conflicts. This step-by-step process involves identifying the conflict, understanding its nature, facilitating open communication, actively solving the issue, and learning from the experience for future reference.

9.9. Integrating Conscious Collaboration in Conflict Resolution

After understanding the conscious approach to conflict resolution, teams need to integrate these principles into their daily work culture. This may entail workshops, dedicated discussions, or bringing in external facilitators. The goal of these efforts should be to help teams understand the value of being mindfully present, empathetic, and respectful even in conflicting situations.

A work environment driven by conscious collaboration does not fear conflict but sees it as a stepping stone towards better understanding, stronger relationships, and improved outcomes. When team members engage consciously and respectfully in conflict resolution, the team can harness the creative power of conflict to soar to new heights of performance and productivity.

Remember, conflict can be the flame that sparks innovation and growth, but it needs the right "wind," the conscious collaboration, to guide its trajectory. With this understanding, you can transform your team, your organization, and ultimately, your shared future.

Chapter 10. The Science Behind Peak Performance

Understanding the concept of peak performance is key to our journey towards conscious collaboration. The myriad facets of peak performance merge the psychological, physiological, and even philosophical aspects of human capability, pushing us towards our utmost potential. It is an experience often described as a state of 'flow' - a harmonious synchronization of mind and body, characterized by an elevated state of concentration and a profound sense of control. This captivating tapestry of intertwined aspects becomes pertinent as we explore the science behind peak performance, delving into the finest threads that contribute to this extraordinary state of function.

10.1. The Mind-Body Connection

Physiologically speaking, peak performance isn't confined to the confines of our cerebral cortex. It rather represents a synergistic relationship between the mind and the body. The brain, our master organ, communicates with every other system in the body, regulating each function. A change in our mental state triggers a cascading influence on our physical state and vice versa. This interplay forms the underlying foundation of peak performance. Through mindfulness training and physical exertion, we can fine-tune this mind-body interaction, driving towards peak performance.

Our autonomic nervous system (ANS), which operates on a subconscious level, plays a crucial role in achieving peak performance. It consists of two components: the sympathetic nervous system, our 'fight or flight' response, and the parasympathetic nervous system, our 'rest and digest' mode. Balancing these systems is key. Too much activation of the sympathetic nervous system can lead to chronic stress and exhaustion. On the other hand, excessive parasympathetic activity can result in complacency and lack of motivation.

By practicing mindfulness and incorporating relaxation techniques such as deep breathing and progressive muscle relaxation, we can modulate our ANS towards an optimal state conducive to peak performance.

10.2. Biochemical Players

Part and parcel of the mind-body dialogue are the biochemical players – neurotransmitters and hormones. These substances are released in response to various triggers and form the communication link within the body. Dopamine, serotonin, oxytocin, and endorphin (known collectively as the 'happiness hormones') each play a role in managing stress, fostering motivation, and ultimately facilitating peak performance.

Evidence suggests that naturally stimulating the release of these hormones, through methods such as exercise, a healthy diet, social interaction, and positive affirmations, helps cultivate an optimal mental and emotional environment.

Not to be overlooked is the hormone cortisol, often cited as the 'stress hormone'. While high levels of chronic cortisol are detrimental, research indicates that acute, manageable stressors leading to temporary cortisol spikes can be leveraged for positive reinforcement, meaning stress, when harnessed appropriately, can catalyze peak performance.

10.3. The Role of Psychological Factors and Positive Affirmations

Psychological elements such as self-confidence, motivation, and resilience are vital to achieving peak performance. These elements are intertwined, each influencing and being influenced by the others in a cyclical interaction.

Self-confidence enhances our belief in ourselves, enabling us to face challenges optimistically. It is nurtured by accomplishing small, realistic goals, receiving positive feedback, and engaging in self-reflection.

Motivation, internal and external, drives us towards our goals. Internal or intrinsic motivators like self-improvement and passion are generally more sustainable than external motivators like rewards or recognition.

Lastly, the quality of resilience allows us to recover from setbacks and persist in our efforts towards peak performance.

10.4. Conscious Collaboration: The Crucial Link

Conscious collaboration is where peak performance steers towards a team-oriented perspective. It elevates the individual-focused peak performance to a collective one by intertwining emotional intelligence, active listening, and respectful communication. Through empathy and understanding, conscious collaboration fosters a culture of mutual trust and shared goals.

Scientifically, group flow, similar to the individual flow state, plays a crucial role in collaborative peak performance. It promotes a shared state of deep engagement and synchronized effort. Research shows that brainwaves of individuals in a successful team sync up during group tasks, exhibiting an actual physical manifestation of 'being on the same page'.

Resonant leadership, characterized by emotional intelligence and empathy, further accelerates team performance. They pave the way for a supportive environment that encourages risk-taking and values contribution, fueling the collective journey towards peak performance.

10.5. A Culture of Learning for Performance

Finally, an atmosphere encouraging continual learning and growth also bolsters peak performance. Such environments enable individuals to expand their capabilities, complementing the drive for personal development and communal progress.

Overall, peak performance stems from the intricate interplay of mind and body, biochemistry, psychology, and collaborative effort. By illuminating and harnessing these scientific insights, we can recalibrate and align towards a culture brimming with peak performance, individually, and through conscious collaboration. It becomes less about excelling at a task, more about nurturing an ecosystem that brings out the best in every individual as part of an extraordinary collective.

Chapter 11. Sustaining Conscious Collaboration for Long Haul Success

Maintaining and fortifying a culture of conscious collaboration for long-term success is both an art and a requirement. When harnessed correctly, it has the potential to elevate your team's performance, spur innovation, and boost overall business results. Yet, it's not a 'set it and forget it' process. What you initiate today must be nurtured and guided with deliberation and intention, growing ever-evolving as your team and business does. Let's explore how!

11.1. The Importance of Nurturing Conscious Collaboration

Conscious collaboration isn't a concept that can merely be implemented and left to its own devices. Instead, it demands regular and meticulous nurturing. This involves constantly promoting and reinforcing the practices that foster an environment of empathy, active listening, profound respect, and shared ambitions. Nurturing conscious collaboration extends to all levels, from individual contributors to management, and it is vital that everyone in the organization understands, embraces, and commits to these principles.

11.2. Continual Reinforcement of Collaborative Principles

One of the most effective ways of nurturing conscious collaboration is by continuously reinforcing its guiding principles. Encourage open communication, emphasize the power of diversity in thought and approach, and insist upon the commitment to common goals. These fundamental principles should not merely be discussed but demonstrated via actions and decisions, thereby giving the concept its deserved embodiment. Regular team-building exercises and events will help to sustain the collaborative mindset, ensuring the principles are integrated into everyday work routines.

11.3. Building Empathy within the Team

Building empathy is a critical aspect of sustaining collaboration. When team members understand and genuinely care for each other, they work better together, leading to improved performance. Empathy can be fostered through regular interpersonal interactions and team-building activities. Instituting programs such as employee mentoring, rotational assignments, and job shadowing can help team members gain a deeper understanding of their colleagues' roles, challenges, and expectations, resulting in increased empathy and mutual respect.

11.4. Encouraging Active Listening

Active listening is another key tenet of conscious collaboration that must be encouraged continually. Be it team meetings, brainstorming sessions, or one-on-one discussions, make active listening a common practice. Encourage everyone in the team to fully engage, understand, and consider their colleagues' perspectives before formulating responses or judgments. Regular training and workshops emphasizing the importance of active listening helps to further integrate this principle into the team's communication habits.

11.5. Promoting Respect and Shared Ambition

In an environment where respect is given freely, and everyone shares a common goal, conscious collaboration thrives. Underpin the importance of treating every team member with unwavering respect, regardless of their role or seniority level. Also, ensure that the team aligns towards shared objectives, each individual understanding their part in achieving the collective ambition. Regular meetings to review and refresh these shared goals can help maintain motivation and commitment.

11.6. Review and Adaptation of Conscious Collaboration Practices

Over time, your methodology for sustaining conscious collaboration needs to evolve. Conscious collaboration isn't a static concept; it requires constant review and adaptation based on team dynamics, business changes, results achieved, and feedback from team members. Regularly review your existing practices in team meetings or dedicated feedback sessions. Adapt and modify the strategies based on these inputs to ensure your collaboration practices are always in line with your team's needs and the overarching business objectives.

11.7. Measuring Success and Addressing Failures

Sustaining conscious collaboration also includes keeping track of its successes and addressing the failures. Success can be measured quantitatively through the achievement of team goals or qualitatively by gauging the improvement in team dynamics, communication, and overall work satisfaction. When there are setbacks or failures, address them openly and honestly. Encourage team members to view these as opportunities for learning and improvement rather than a chance for blame.

11.8. Conclusion: Sustaining Conscious Collaboration — A Continuous Endeavor

Building upon the essence of nurturing conscious collaboration, remember that it is a continuous endeavor. It requires constant reaffirmation of the principles and values it champions. It's a means to unite the team in a common purpose, promoting empathy and respect throughout. As your team grows and the dynamics change, your practices may need to adjust. Regardless, by approaching conscious collaboration as a long-term commitment to your team's overall success, you can drive impressive business results, encourage innovation, and create a thriving work culture.

In conclusion, sustaining conscious collaboration is a worthwhile investment for teams. It presents a path towards a comprehensive and inclusive work culture that extends beyond revenues and productivity to shape a purposeful professional community, relentlessly striving for shared successes. Your conscious collaboration strategies are your team's guiding light, leading them towards a fulfilling, engaging, and successful professional journey.

www.ingramcontent.com/pod-product-compliance
Lightning Source LLC
Chambersburg PA
CBHW071013260726
48661CB00007B/2940